Excelling In Character

A Study Of The Book of Titus

By

Christina Williams

Excelling In Character

A Study Of The Book of Titus

By:

Christina Williams

Published By:

ABM Publications

A division of Andrew Bills Ministries, Inc.
PO Box 6811, Orange, CA 92863
www.abmpublications.com

ISBN: 978-1-931820-33-2

DEDICATION

Dedicated to my wonderful husband Grady, a godly leader and amazing husband, who I think of when I think of someone excelling in character.

Also, to the amazing people who have modeled a walk with Christ in integrity and truth in my life. There are so many of you; too many to name individually, but you have impacted my life in an eternal way and for that I am truly grateful.

Special thanks to my wonderful son, Chris Williams, for the beautiful cover design on this book.

To Andrew Bills, for the publishing this book, to whom I am so grateful.

Additionally, to those of you who will model integrity and excellent character for others in the future, this is dedicated to you. On behalf of those who will learn from your example, thank you.

TABLE OF CONTENTS

ACKNOWLEDGEMENTS

Our Group at Sunrise Christian Fellowship used the Titus Bible Study by Christina Williams. This study was not only so informative but produced deep and lively discussion when we went into our groups. Christina's knowledge and love of God enabled the women to go home and apply God's word and teaching into our own lives. As a Pastor's wife and leader of our women's ministry, I highly recommend this Study.

Shellie Richardson, Sunrise Christian Fellowship

Christina, thank you for all your work to provide us with the Bible Study on Titus. I really like Book Studies because the focus is on the Word. This one was very thorough and well done. It provided thought provoking questions which resulted in a lot of good discussion among the women that attended. Thanks.

Carrie Becker, Leader and Teacher

FORWARD

Christina Williams has the incredible ability to pull truths from God's Word in such a way that the reader can attain them, understand them and be transformed by them. I highly recommend this study on Titus as Christina is a strong woman of faith and a powerful teacher of Scripture.

Dr. Patti Helzer
Founder of Mourning to Morning Ministries

II Corinthians 5:17 says, "If any man be in Christ, he is a new creature, old things are passed away, behold all things are become new." No matter what a person has previously experienced, we must not allow our past to enslave us to negative thoughts, unforgiveness, ungodly enticements or destructive allurements. With the assistance of The Holy Spirit, we as believers must arise and walk in obedience and in the characteristics mentioned in the fruit of The Spirit, as recorded in Galatians Chapter 5.

Not only does Christina Williams' book on Titus reveal this, but it ensures us that our past sorrows can become our strong points as we turn to Christ

and live in the power of The Holy Spirit of God. As
ambassadors of Christ, we are to be examples or
role models of His Grace. Her book has been
published as an encouragement to demonstrate
that through faith in God, you can arise, stand and
be a pattern for others to follow, so they too may
walk in the victory that Christ Jesus has given us.

Andrew Bills
Pastor/Evangelist of The Victory Report Hour
International Ministries and the president of ABM
Publications.

PREFACE

I love the Word of God! It has healed me, delivered me, inspired me, taught me, comforted me and never ceases to bring me daily revelation. Out of this great passion for the Word of God I wrote this study.

This study of the book of Titus, originally was written for a group Bible Study, but I have arranged it now that you could do this as an individual or as a group.

My hope as you go through this study that you will fall passionately in love with God and His written word as I have and that you will want to apply it daily to your life. In the end if the words stay on the page and are not applied into every aspect of your life, they are meaningless. However, if they come alive in and through you, it will astound you when you begin to see what God will do through your obedience.

May our Lord Jesus Christ give you an intense passion for the Word of God and His heart for the people in your world. Mostly, may He be glorified through our lives lived for Him.

INTRODUCTION

Looking for role models that live a life worth following? Needing to find the truth in a world of lies? Trying to find a way to live in a culture that wants nothing to do with God?

This practical Bible study on the book of Titus study will help you live an honest life loving God and the people around you.

This book looks at a letter from a mentor teaching a young leader how to live in a complicated culture with integrity and character. Today we need that advice more than ever, this book will help a significant letter from the Apostle Paul come alive and become applicable to your life today.

Discover a way to excel in character and to live a life doing good for the people in your world.

Chapter 1

Living What You Learn

*Be diligent to present yourself approved to God,
a worker who does not need to be ashamed,
rightly dividing the word of truth.
2 Timothy 2:1 NKJ*

What kind of people do we find in the Church? Often we can find ourselves shocked at the behavior of people who we go to Church with. We may have heard recently in the news, some horrific indiscretion of a Pastor to the devastation of his family, Church, and community.

Or, you might find yourself shocked at rude or mean-spirited behavior professing Christians can display, in or outside the Church. Ethics and honesty might be more present in those professing no faith in God. This type of behavior gives such a poor representation of Christ and the transformation He can bring to our character if we allow Him to.

In writing this letter to Titus the Apostle Paul knew that the people in Church didn't just need to hear about Jesus, it needed to be lived out among them. It had to start with those who wanted to be leaders, living in an intimate relationship with the living God themselves. Then revealing, to those around them, a new, radical, lifestyle of love and honor which is the fruit of living loving relationship with God.

Paul knew that his days were few, and he needed to prepare and train leaders for the future of the Church. In the book of Titus, he details the qualities of a dynamic leader, warning that pastors, elders and deacons hold a tremendous responsibility in guiding their flocks in the true gospel.

Paul believed it was crucial that church leaders 'walk the talk.' This would be a vital difference in those who followed Christ versus those who lived in bondage to the law. He was calling people to not simply 'know' the law but to live a life of intimacy and love for God and for people.

He warns us in this book about false teachers and those who have no character. Leaders and teachers who simply want to bring division into the Church and deceive and confuse many people. Such people have no redemptive character and are self-seeking and divisive.

Paul encourages the readers of this letter to have our character redeemed and to then disciple others. Truly living the great commission. (Matthew 28:19)

Let's learn some facts about the book of Titus.

The Author of Book of Titus:
The Apostle Paul written from Macedonia

Date Written:
Scholars date this Pastoral Epistle to around 64 A.D. Most scholars feel it was just a few years before he was martyred by order of the Roman Emperor Nero.

Written To:
Titus, was a Greek Christian and young Pastor whom Paul entrusted to oversee the churches on the island of Crete. These instructions on faith and behavior are particularly relevant in any society struggling with immorality, so they could apply to churches and Christians today.

Context of the Book of Titus:

Titus served churches on the island of Crete, in the Mediterranean Sea south of Greece. Crete was notorious in ancient times for immorality, quarreling, and laziness. Paul had probably planted these churches, and he was concerned about filling them with leaders who were people of honor and integrity, living as good examples as followers of Christ.

Themes in the Book of Titus:
• Faithfully following the gospel leads to godly character and behaviour. If a person believes in Christ, their actions will reflect those beliefs. Good works do not save us, but they do reflect our heart and relationship with God.

• Today the church's survival depends on having godly people serve as pastors and elders. Their response to God can serve as examples that lead others to the gospel. Paul lists several qualities of effective leaders. Christians should be good citizens, obeying the laws and treating everyone with kindness. They should devote themselves to good works.

Key Verses:

Titus 1:7-9

An elder is a manager of God's household, so he must live a blameless life. He must not be arrogant or quick-tempered; he must not be a heavy drinker, violent, or dishonest with money. 8 Rather, he must enjoy having guests in his home, and he must love what is good. He must live wisely and be just. He must live a devout and disciplined life. 9 He must have a strong belief in the trustworthy message he was taught; then he will be able to encourage others with wholesome teaching and show those who oppose it where they are wrong. NLT

Titus 2:11-14

For the grace of God has been revealed, bringing salvation to all people. And we are instructed to turn from godless living and sinful pleasures. We should live in this evil world with wisdom, righteousness, and devotion to God, 13 while we look forward with hope to that wonderful day when the glory of our great God and Savior, Jesus Christ, will be revealed. 14 He gave his life to free us from every kind of sin, to cleanse us, and to make us his very own people, totally committed to doing good deeds.NLT

Titus 3:1-2

Remind the believers to submit to the government and its officers. They should be obedient, always ready to do what is good. 2 They must not slander anyone and must avoid quarreling. Instead, they should be gentle and show true humility to everyone.NLT

Titus 3:3 - 7
For we ourselves were once foolish, disobedient, led astray, slaves to various passions and pleasures, passing our days in malice and envy, hated by others and hating one another. 4 But when the goodness and loving kindness of God our Savior appeared, 5 He saved us, not because of works done by us in righteousness, but according to His own mercy, the washing of regeneration and renewal of the Holy Spirit,6 whom He poured out on us richly through Jesus Christ our Savior, 7 so that being justified by his grace we might become heirs according to the hope of eternal life.ESV

Titus 3:9-11
But avoid foolish controversies, genealogies, dissensions, and quarrels about the law, for they are unprofitable and worthless. 10 As for a person who stirs up division, after warning him once and then twice, have nothing more to do with him, 11 knowing that such a person is warped and sinful; he is self-condemned. ESV

Take some time to answer these questions.

1) If you were going to give advice on character and living as a Christian as Paul did to Titus to someone younger than you, what would it be?

_____

_____

_____

_____

2) Look up... Matthew 28:19, 20

What is God teaching you to obey that could be passed on to others?

_____

_____

_____

_____

3) If teaching others is a command what does this scripture say to you.....

John 10:10 NIV, If you keep my commands, you will remain in my love, just as I have kept my Father's commands and remain in his love.

_____

_____

_____

_____

4) Who has God put in your life to teach or
   disciple?

_____

_____

_____

_____

End your time asking God to show you who
your disciples are and how you can be
obedient to the command of Christ.

This week's verse to meditate on and memorize is one of the key verses:

For the grace of God has been revealed, bringing
salvation to all people. And we are instructed to
turn from godless living and sinful pleasures. We
should live in this evil world with wisdom,
righteousness, and devotion to God, while we
look forward with hope to that wonderful day
when the glory of our great God and Savior, Jesus
Christ, will be revealed.

He gave his life to free us from every kind of sin,
to cleanse us, and to make us his very own
people, totally committed to doing good deeds
Titus 2:11-14 NLT

Chapter 2

Who Am I and What Am I Doing?

I, Paul, am God's slave and Christ's agent for promoting the faith among God's chosen people, getting out the accurate word on God and how to respond rightly to it. My aim is to raise hopes by pointing the way to life without end. Titus 1:1

This simple question can be one of the most difficult to answer. Knowing who we in Christ and why are we here is essential for our ability to function effectively and in confidence. Although these seem like straightforward questions, many of us are so beaten down by this life they are the hardest to answer. What happens to most of us is our identity in Christ gets robbed from us, then we end up making poor decisions based on a feeling of worthlessness.

In a love relationship with the living God, we can truly find our identity and purpose as God reveals His love for us, even in our broken state. When we understand how dearly God loves us and our intrinsic value, we are less likely to look for affirmation from people. Looking for our personal self worth from people is never fruitful and always demoralizing. However, finding our value and gifting, as a result of growing in Christ has daily surprises and satisfaction.

One of my favorite scriptures is Jeremiah 17. It helps remind me where to put my trust and faith, and what my life is like when I put all my hope in what flesh can do for me:

Jeremiah 17:5-8
"This is what the Lord says: "Cursed are those who put their trust in mere humans, who rely on human strength and turn their hearts away from the Lord.
6 They are like stunted shrubs in the desert, with no hope for the future. They will live in the barren wilderness, in an uninhabited salty land.
7 "But blessed are those who trust in the Lord and have made the Lord their hope and confidence.
8 They are like trees planted along a riverbank, with roots that reach deep into the water. Such trees are not bothered by the heat or worried by long months of drought. Their leaves stay green, and they never stop producing fruit." NLT

So we have to remind ourselves on a daily that our confidence comes from a relationship with God and then we will never stop seeing the good fruit of that in our lives. In my own life, this has become an essential part of my existence as God continually puts me into situations where I feel helpless unless I have His strength and power. I am keenly aware that man is not my answer and that if God is the only one who can restore and redeem my life otherwise I have nothing. According to Jeremiah and Paul that is a blessed place.

Paul starts off this letter declaring exactly who he is and what he is created by God to do.

Titus 1:1
This letter is from Paul, a slave of God and an apostle of Jesus Christ.

Paul has elevated the position of servant, or slave as stated in the New Living Translation, to a height greater than Apostle. In most cultures, any title that someone could have would be revered greater than that of a slave or servant. Paul states that with all the titles he held, holds that of a servant of Christ in the greatest esteem by stating it first, before that of Apostle.

Look at the scriptures and see if this was just generous talk.

Matthew 12:18

Matthew 20:25-28

Matthew 23:11

Mark 9:35

Mark 10:43

Luke 22:25-27

Titus 1:1 - 3

I have been sent to proclaim faith to those God has chosen and to teach them to know the truth that shows them how to live godly lives. 2 This truth gives them confidence that they have eternal life, which God—who does not lie—promised them before the world began. 3 And now at just the right time He has revealed this message, which we announce to everyone. It is by the command of God our Savior that I have been entrusted with this work for him.

Paul is concise here, understanding who he is and what he has been called to do and the significance of what he does in impacting other believers. He walks humbly and yet with great confidence in what he is created to do and why he is doing it. As believers, our identity and purpose are significant, and yet too often that is the very thing that has been robbed from us. Our significance. It is easy to sink into the lie of believing you are insignificant, but nothing is further from the truth.

I love this scripture in The New Living Translation...

1 Peter 2:10
"Once you had no identity as a people; now you are God's people. Once you received no mercy; now you have received God's mercy."

As you look up the following scriptures, ask God to reveal to you who you are in Christ and the significance of what you are created to do.

Jeremiah 29:11

Hosea 2:23

Luke 12:7

Matthew 10:31

Romans 15:2-6

Ephesians 2:10

1 Thessalonians 5:11

_____
_____
_____
_____

More than the work that God does in you - is the work He does through you, and the impact of your life on the lives of those God has put around you. Paul is clear that as he serves and obeys the Lord, his life has an eternal effect on everyone who comes in contact with him.

Titus 1:2 & 3 states, "This truth gives them confidence that they have eternal life, which God—who does not lie—promised them before the world began. 3 And now at just the right time He has revealed this message, which we announce to everyone." He was clear that his purpose now was to announce to everyone that he had found eternal life.

According to Paul when we speak the truth of what God is doing in our lives, we give confidence to others. As believers, we are asked to announce or proclaim the truth of God's words to the people in our world. Too often we are quick to speak our own words or thoughts, which can misrepresent Christ and mess things up. Yet Paul is clear about his message and the importance of it.

What are we being asked to do and to announce according to God's word?

1 Corinthians 10:23 - 24

2 Corinthians 12:19

Ephesians 4:20 – 32

_____

_____

_____

_____

In Titus 1: 4 Paul says, " May God the Father and Christ Jesus our Savior give you grace and peace". Paul states fervently that his life depended on the grace and mercy of God. Too often we forget what Paul knew and think that it is something we have done, or earned, in our life by living good. In truth, we are extremely dependent on the grace and peace of God in our lives.

What robs you of living in grace and peace?

_____

_____

_____

_____

Where do we obtain grace and peace?

John 10:10

2 Thessalonians 1:2

_____

_____

_____

_____

What can we do to live more in Grace and Peace?

Philippians 4:6 -7

Colossians 3:12-17

John 14:27

Romans 5:1-5

Romans 8:5-8
Ephesians 2:14-22

_____

_____

_____

_____

Meditate on and memorize this verse, Luke 1:79:

This verse tells us that Jesus' purpose was to guide those of us who live in darkness to a path of peace. Pray that you will learn how to walk in peace in your life in a new way, asking God to guide your feet to a full knowledge of who you are in Him and your incredible value.

Through the heartfelt mercies of our God,
God's Sunrise will break in upon us,
Shining on those in the darkness,
those sitting in the shadow of death,
Then showing us the way, one foot at a time,
down the path of peace. Luke 1:79

Chapter 3

Character Counts

*I left you in charge in Crete so you
could complete what I left half-done.
Appoint leaders in every town according to
my instructions. As you select them, ask,
"Is this man well-thought-of?
Titus 1:5*

I remember years ago, Robert Clinton from Fuller Theological Seminary coming to speak to us as Pastors, and he kept saying to us, 'few leaders finish well.'

What he was saying is, you can start out great and looking good, but as the years go by and trouble comes, can you sustain it? Leadership and the character of a leader are important to God. As Paul was writing to Titus about setting leaders in place in this young Church, it is clear he is telling Titus to look for a person who is already living as a leader, not someone who could follow a list of rules so that he can become or look like a leader.

Too often people can make themselves look good to 'get the job', and then let down once they are in place of authority. We have sometimes seen in our experiance in the Church, that person will become a leader and then think their lifestyle doesn't have to be consistent to keep them there. I believe that if you put leaders into place that are already living as a leader, without a title or position, they are more likely going to continue what they were doing once they have a title.

When I was in college, I wrote a paper for my Church Administration course called, "To Be or Not To Be - Ordained." My position on Ordination was that I would serve the same with or without a title. (the school I went to was yet undecided on this issue) What mattered to me was not a title, but that I was daily walking in obedience to God.

Look at Titus 1:5-9 and see how many of the qualifications are character and integrity issues. How this person lived out their faith at home, became an essential qualification for leadership.

"For this reason I left you in Crete, that you should set in order the things that are lacking, and appoint elders in every city as I commanded you— if a man is blameless, the husband of one wife, having faithful children not accused of dissipation or insubordination. For a bishop must be blameless, as a steward of God, not self-willed, not quick-tempered, not given to wine, not violent, not greedy for money, but hospitable, a lover of what is good, sober-minded, just, holy, self-controlled, holding fast the faithful word as he has been taught, that he may be able, by sound doctrine, both to exhort and convict those who contradict."

_____

_____

_____

_____

Look at the following scriptures and see how God chose leaders.

1 Samuel 16:7

Luke 6:12, 13

_____

_____

_____

_____

What are leaders asked to do?

Ephesians 4:11-32

_____

_____

_____

_____

With that in mind it is understandable that God would prompt Paul to set character qualities upon leaders in the new Church. Character is what sets leaders apart and makes them worthy to follow. It is interesting that these characteristics are how a leader lives at home and the fruit from a lifestyle of living in the Spirit. Anyone can put a show on for a few hours in church on Sunday but how we live in our homes sets us apart in the sight of God.

Look at the lists in Galatians 5: 19 -26 and compare the evidence of living in the flesh and the fruit of the Spirit.

_____

_____

_____

_____

If Titus was to look for these qualities, do these come from striving to be perfect?

Romans 7:18
John 3:6

I Peter 1:2

Ezekiel 36:26-27

Zechariah 4:6

_____
_____
_____
_____

Is Paul asking people to live under a new set of rules? Legalism was the basis of religion for the Pharisees and the very thing Paul addressed in his letter to the Galatians. Pharisees lived very proud that they followed the Law to the letter, and yet they were the ones Jesus rebuked, not those who knew they were sinners. So a strict adherence to a set of rules is clearly not what pleases God. **What do the following scriptures tell you regarding this?**

Galatians 2:16

Galatians 3:22 - 24

Philippians 3:12-14
Romans 7:6

_____

_____

_____

_____

So how are we to walk in a way that is pleasing to God?

Galatians 5:1

Ephesians 5:8-10

John 14:26

Romans 8:1 - 14

_____

_____

_____

_____

The Holy Spirit will change our attitude and character if we allow Him to. I remember once not wanting to attend a Conference in our area that I knew I needed to go to as a leader so others would support it. I realized I had a bad attitude, so as I prayed about this I knew that the only way to break this was to serve.

I offered to do whatever they needed at this Conference, even though I had a busy schedule, I knew this attitude had to change. When I laid down my desires and became a servant to people, God, who saw my heart, not only changed my attitude, but developed my character into the leader He wanted me to be.

Look again at Galatians 5:19 - 26 and see that is the Holy Spirit, who changes our nature and character. Where we might have been too proud to apologize when we live according to the Spirit of God, He will draw us to repentance and humility. Not by adherence to the Law that says, 'Thou shalt not" but by an intimate love relationship with God, where are we transformed and pleasing to God.

So are we called to look for leaders who are perfect according to this list Paul gave Titus? Or are we simply to walk according to the Spirit and then look for leaders are are showing us the way to do that by the example of their lives lived before God?

_____

_____

_____

_____

Pray and ask the Lord to help you draw closer to Him, to hear His voice, and to help you live in a way that is pleasing to Him. To truly make Him Lord of your life and to help you be obedient to the voice of the Holy Spirit as He transforms your nature and character.

Meditate on and memorize this verse:

For once you were full of darkness, but now you have light from the Lord. So live as people of light! For this light within you produces only what is good and right and true. Carefully determine what pleases the Lord.
Ephesians 5:8-10 NLT

Chapter 4

Excelling in Character

I left you in charge in Crete so you could complete what I left half-done. Appoint leaders in every town according to my instructions. As you select them, ask, "Is this man well-thought-of?
Titus 1:5,6

Living in Grace and Truth

If we want to become a true follower of Christ we are supposed to become more and more like Jesus, living and loving as He did. **John 1:14** tells us that Jesus was full of grace and truth.

He encourages His disciples to understand that they are to teach everything He has commanded them. Paul thoroughly comprehended this as he taught about the character of leaders to Titus. He continues to write about what he was asking Titus to look for in a good leader.

Jesus revealed how a leader should walk in uncompromising truth but with abundant grace for everyone we meet. One of my favorite examples is the encounter with the Samaritan woman at the well. **(John Chapter 4)** Jesus tells her the absolute truth about her trail of broken relationships and then commends her for being honest, when she says, 'I have no husband.' He had so much grace for a woman whose life experience had most likely not earned much of that from her lifestyle.

Look at the following scriptures and write down what you learned about the character of Christ.

John 1:14-18

Psalm 45:2

Psalms 25:10

Ephesians 2:8,9

John 14:6

_____
_____
_____
_____

Because He is full of Grace and truth, what are we to do?

Proverbs 3:1-4

Proverbs 22:11

Psalm 40:10

Psalm 51:6

Romans 14:19

2 Corinthians 12:9

_____
_____
_____
_____

Paul warned Titus about rebellious leaders who then would in turn confuse others. Based on what we have been discussing look at the following scripture and find the characteristics of the leaders he warned him about.

Titus 1:10-16
There are many people who refuse to cooperate, who talk about worthless things and lead others into the wrong way—mainly those who insist on circumcision to be saved. 11 These people must be stopped, because they are upsetting whole families by teaching things they should not teach, which they do to get rich by cheating people.12

Even one of their own prophets said, "Cretans are always liars, evil animals, and lazy people who do nothing but eat." 13 The words that prophet said are true. So firmly tell those people they are wrong so they may become strong in the faith, 14 not accepting Jewish false stories and the commands of people who reject the truth. 15 To those who are pure, all things are pure, but to those who are full of sin and do not believe, nothing is pure. Both their minds and their consciences have been ruined. 16 They say they know God, but their actions show they do not accept him. They are hateful people, they refuse to obey, and they are useless for doing anything good.

Interesting that he links those insisting on the circumcision of all believers into this group of wrong leaders. Paul firmly taught that leaders who insist on our ability to conform to the law as a means of salvation took away from the complete work of Christ on the cross. It was a battle for freedom in Christ Paul was willing to fight.

Look at Acts 15: 1, 2, 6-11. Peter makes an important statement in verse 11. What significance is that to you?

_____
_____
_____
_____

Paul is letting us see in this letter to Titus, that insisting on circumcision is exactly what Peter is talking about when he said, *'laying on them a burden that neither they or their ancestors were able to bear."*

He is concerned about these leaders because instead of leading people into freedom and truth, they lead them into rules and bondage. Jesus warned about this as well when he said, *"beware of the yeast of the Pharisees and Sadducee's."*
,
One of their own leaders says, in a truthful statement about their nature when *'they are liars and lazy'*? Is Titus instructed to reject them because of this? No, Paul instructs Titus to tell them they are wrong, so they may become strong in truth. Thank God there is hope for our lazy, sinful nature!

By becoming proficient in our faith and not living by a list of 'false stories and commands of people,' we can become pure and walk in the truth.

What are some of the ways we can grow into someone who is walking in truth and not stay remain in a sinful, lazy nature?

Proverbs 3:3-7

Proverbs 15:1-3

Proverbs 26:3-12

Psalm 86:11-13

Psalm 119:30-32 & 43-48

_____
_____
_____
_____

Ask God to help you become a seeker of truth walking not according to rules and laws, but as Jesus walked *'full of grace and truth.'* The challenge this week is that as you walk in truth and grace from God for yourself, extend that to the people around you. Write down any opportunities you are given to show grace and truth this next week. I know whenever I have the privilege of extending grace to someone, it shocks them because they expect judgement and condemnation. I love that it is the heart of our Father to extend grace and mercy. As Paul says here in Titus *"to the pure, all things are pure"* let's continue to reveal the pure love and grace of God this week to the world around us.

Meditate on and memorize these verses:

The Lord is close to all who call on him, yes, to all who call on him in truth.
Psalm 145:18

You shall know the truth and the truth will set you free.
John 8:32

Chapter 5

How Should You Live?

"Everything is pure to those whose hearts are pure. But nothing is pure to those who are corrupt and unbelieving, because their minds and consciences are corrupted. Such people claim they know God, but they deny him by the way they live. They are detestable and disobedient, worthless for doing anything good."   *Titus 1:15 -16 NLT*

One of the most common complaints against the Church is, 'they are all hypocrites.' (Which I have to laugh and say, "Of course there are no hypocrites in bars or at ballgames!")

However, those who complain about people who are proclaiming to follow God and yet live the opposite way entirely are in good company.

Jesus felt the same way when he rebuked the Pharisees and Paul felt the same way here. It is refreshing when we meet someone who is authentically living what they preach and are genuine in how they treat people revealing the character and nature Christ. As we look at the end of **Titus 1**, the challenge is to live with a pure heart.

Look at the following scriptures, and with an understanding of living with a pure heart, write down what you would say to a young disciple.

Psalm 18:26

2 Samuel 22:25-27

Proverbs 3:34

Proverbs 21:8

_____
_____
_____
_____

Look at Proverb 6:12 - 19 to get the heart of God regarding a wrong way of living. After looking at this portion of scripture, what are the things you hear regarding how to live with a pure heart?

_____
_____
_____
_____

So many people say they know God but are living in such a way that denies God, as we begin

Chapter 2 of Titus Paul clearly instructs Titus in the way he should live.

Titus 2:1

As for you, Titus, promote the kind of living that reflects wholesome teaching. New Living Version

Titus is encouraged not to be a religious hypocrite but to live, in a way, that reflects right teaching. Living a lifestyle that is worthy of a man of God. The Amplified Bible says this wonderfully.

Titus 2:1

But [as for] you, teach what is fitting and becoming to sound (wholesome) doctrine [the character and right living that identify true Christians]. Amplified

Paul then goes on to say what right teaching is and how it should manifest in the lives of men and women.

Being taught good sound Biblical doctrine is not enough, it needs to manifest itself in how we live.

Write down what the following scriptures say to you about how right teaching should manifest itself in our lives.

James 1:22

James 4:17

Luke 6:46-48

Luke 11:28

Romans 2:13

_____
_____
_____
_____

So attending Church and Bible Study is a great beginning but the Word of God needs to birth obedience in us and change the way we live. **Psalm 119:11**

One Sunday afternoon we met a Pastor for lunch in a nearby town and after many problems in the restaurant with our order and our table, the waitress exclaimed, 'you are really nice for a Sunday group'. We asked what she meant by that and were informed that no one wanted to work on Sundays because, (in her words, not mine) "We are not sure what happens to people in Church, but by the time they get here, they are mean!"

We told her we were Pastors and gave her our assurance that our congregations would hear about this! What a terrible statement in that community the Christians had earned for themselves.

What are these scriptures asking us to do? What do you need to do to make that happen?

3 John 1:11

Galatians 6:7 - 10

2 Timothy 3: 10 - 17

Colossians 3:17

_____

_____

_____

_____

As you conclude this chapter, ask God to help you truly hear His Word and to walk in obedience to it. Think of one thing this week that you will ask God to work in your life that will reveal that you are someone 'promoting the right kind of living'.

Meditate on and memorize this verse:

My life is an example to many, because you have been my strength and protection.   Psalm 71:7

Chapter 6

Essentials

*As for you, Titus, promote the kind of living
that reflects wholesome teaching.
Titus 2:1 New Living Translation*

Sam Jones a dynamic southern evangelist (1847-1906) whose acclaim rose to national limelight in 1885. Sam was both a national figure as well as a devoted family man. His wife, Laura Jones, wrote about the fact that he had a great love for his family as well receiving popularity in public life. *"Although I can not express in words what he was to me or how I loved him, I want the world to know, as many thousands already know that he was the greatest man of the nineteenth century in public life - pure, honorable, and kind to all his fellow men - his greatness was in greater evidence in the place loved above all else - his home....I knew him in his faithfulness to God"*

We have been looking at the heart of a true believer revealed in how he lives not just what he professes or how he or she can look to others. In the development of real Christian character in this Chapter, Paul tells Titus what is essential to instruct, and then breaks it down to stages of life, and the Christian character traits to teach on. The list is impressive as Paul gives thoughts on what to teach older men.

Titus 2: 2

Teach the older men to exercise self-control, to be worthy of respect, and to live wisely. They must have sound faith and be filled with love and patience.

Self Control - means restraint exercised over one's own impulses, emotions, or desires. If more people were taught to exercise self-control, it would have a significant and positive impact on their families and communities. It would truly reveal the work of Christ in lives yielded to Him.

We also saw in Galatians 5:22 that self-control is a fruit, or evidence, that the Holy Spirit is at work in your life. If we are willing, God will give us self-control, through the power of the Holy Spirit.

As a young believer, I watched a leader I admired just have a glass of water at a restaurant with a table of dignitaries asking him to eat. He repeatedly declined and afterward I asked privately why he didn't eat, he told me that he was fasting. Although fasting was a new concept to me, what impressed me was that God had given him self-control in that situation.

Look at the following scriptures and write down what they are saying to you about the importance of self-control.

Proverbs 16:32

Romans 8:11-14

1 Peter 2:9 - 12

 Proverbs 25:28

1 Corinthians 9:27

_____

_____

_____

_____

Self Control reveals itself in the maturity of the believer as they learn to live conscious of the needs of others not just their own.

Titus 2:2 says, in the New Living Version, that a man should be taught 'to be 'worthy of respect,' not to require people to honor you.

In the New King Version **Titus 2:2** reads," *that the older men be sober, reverent, temperate, sound in faith, in love, in patience*;

What I love about these qualities is that if a man lives according to this teaching it will be very easy to respect and honor him. Laura Jones went on to say how fortunate she was to be a part of Sam Jones' life as his wife, because everyone else knew a powerful preacher, but she knew a man who truly lived what he preached.

What would those who are living with you say they see in you?

_____
_____
_____
_____

Looking at the following scriptures, what is this saying to you about how you should live?

2 Peter 1:5 - 9

Philippians 4:8-9

_____
_____
_____
_____

What ways are you living true to what you say?

_____

_____

_____

_____

What area do you need to ask the Holy Spirit to give you self - control?

_____

_____

_____

_____

Then in **verse 3** Paul says, " _Likewise, teach the older women to be reverent in the way they live, not to be slanderers or addicted to much wine, but to teach what is good_" New Living Version

Notice that older women, as the men do, need to watch the way they live, not being slanderers or defamers.

The word 'slanderer' in the Greek is the same word used for the Satan, diabolos, is also used in scripture for false accuser and the devil. Paul encourages older women not to live as the evil one, who would slander and accuse God's people, but to communicate what is valuable.

As you read the following scriptures, note how God feels about those who would slander one another.

Leviticus 19:16

Psalm 50:16-23

Psalm 101:5

Proverbs 6:16-19

Proverbs 17:4

Proverbs 30:10

Jeremiah 6:27 - 30

Matthew 15:19

Ephesians 4:29-31

Colossians 3:8

_____
_____
_____
_____

After looking at all of these scriptures, you should have a clear understanding of God's feeling about us when we talk badly or slander one another.

As you have studied God's word regarding how to speak about others, ask the Lord to work in your life and give you self-control. When you are tempted to slander another remember what the scriptures have taught you about this type of activity, and how God can give you self-control.

Meditate on and memorize this verse:

Take control of what I say, O Lord, and guard my lips. Don't let me drift toward evil or take part in acts of wickedness. Don't let me share in the delicacies of those who do wrong.
Psalm 141:3,4

Chapter 7

What Do You Teach?

*Guide older women into lives of reverence so they
end up as neither gossips nor drunks,
but models of goodness. By looking at them,
the younger women will know how to love
their husbands and children, be virtuous and pure,
keep a good house, be good wives.
Titus 2:3-5*

There is a familiar story of a young girl cooking a ham with her mother and in preparing the ham, the mother cut the end off. The girl said *'Mom why do you always cut the end off the ham*?', to which the Mother replied, 'I don't know, my Mother always did it that way.' So they decided to call her Grandmother to find out why she had cut the end off the ham in that manner. The Grandmother replied, '*I don't know why you do it; my pan was too small*!'.

Each of us whether we know it or not are teaching others every day, sometimes it is good and sometimes we teach others what not to do. Paul here is encouraging Timothy to teach men and women to be more deliberate about it and what is the best things to pass on.

I love this text in the New Living Version

Titus 2:3-5

"Similarly, teach the older women to live in a way that honors God. They must not slander others or be heavy drinkers. Instead, they should teach others what is good. These older women must train the younger women to love their husbands and their children, to live wisely and be pure, to work in their homes, to do good, and to be submissive to their husbands. Then they will not bring shame on the word of God."

We talked about slander in the last chapter and the significance of not becoming an 'accuser' of others because that was a characteristic of Satan. We can ask the Holy Spirit to work self-control in us to change the way we speak about people so that we do good to others and not evil with our mouths.

Then Paul instructs that older women be taught not to be heavy drinkers, in most older versions of this **Titus 2:3** text it says, not given to too much wine. The word given in the original Greek means 'enslaved or to bring under bondage.' He is instructing and encouraging women to be trained not to become under bondage to too much wine.

Look at the following scriptures and list some of the consequences and warnings of being under bondage to alcohol.

Isaiah 5:11 -12

Proverbs 20:1

Luke 21:34

_____

_____

_____

_____

Paul goes on in **Titus 1:4** to instruct older women to teach younger how to love their husbands. The Greek word here in this text for love is *philandrous*, where we get the word *philanthropy*. (The word *philanthropy* means, '*a desire to promote the welfare of others, by the generous donation of money to good causes.*') This word, *philandrous*, occurs nowhere else in the New Testament, and it means '*affectionate*' or '*with emotion.*' Isn't it interesting that younger woman are to be taught to love their husbands with generous affection and emotion.

In **Ephesians 5:25**, Paul directs husbands to love their wives, and in **Ephesians 5:33**, he instructs wives to reverence or respect their husbands. Here in Titus, he says that a wife should be taught to love with *philandrous* love. This love is different than the word Paul used in the Ephesians texts regarding husbands loving their wives. The word, love in the Ephesians texts for husbands is the Greek word '*agape*', it means to '*love dearly, to be well pleased, to be contented*,' clearly a different word than the word used here in Titus. Paul is asking women to teach or train younger women or wives to love their husbands with generous affection.

As I thought about the need for older women to teach younger women to love their husbands with 'generous affection,' my first thought was,' *you would think that would come naturally*.' However, one of the things I have noticed that can happen to wives of any age is that you can begin to take a spouse for granted. Affection is often the first thing that goes out the window. The fire that might have created the marriage, quickly turns into embers, as the responsibility of marriage douses the flame.

In our Marriage Seminars, **The Secret to Enduring Love**, I talk to women about the importance of affection and intimacy in a healthy marriage. Too often a wife can find herself carrying so much responsibility, that when she sees her husband her first thought is the long list of things he could do to help her. However, the older you get and the longer you stay married, you start to realize that having a good man in your life is a gift, and you begin to put all those responsibilities into perspective. Life becomes more than a list of chores; it becomes filled with gratitude and appreciation of having someone in your life. I think this is the perspective that Paul is instructing older women to teach, to pour out generous love toward the man God has given you, and in that way revealing your gratitude for God's gift to you.

My own father died when I was seven, he was thirty-nine years old and my Mom and Dad were married only 15 years. I learned, at a very young age, to value the people in my life because I never knew how long I would have them. I promised that I would never end a conversation with my husband on the phone or in person without declaring my love for him. I made it a point to make our last words to each other in any conversation, loving words.

Look at the following scriptures and list what the scriptures are saying to you about loving generously and sacrificially with affection.

Proverbs 5:15-19

Proverbs 10:12

Song of Solomon 1:2

I John 4:8

John 13:34,35

John 15:12,13,17

_____
_____
_____
_____

If, as it says in **Proverbs 5:19**, a man needs to be 'enraptured' by the love of his wife, and women to learn to love their husbands with *generous affection* think how differently every home would be if this were lived out on a daily basis.

Ask the Lord to show you ways to be an example of God's generous love to the people around you.

Remember someone is learning from your life!

Meditate on and memorize this verse:

Love prospers when a fault is forgiven, but dwelling on it separates close friends.
Proverbs 17:9

Chapter 8

Living Wisely

A good woman is hard to find, and worth far more than diamonds. Proverbs 31:10

I am so grateful for the women in my life that over the years have taught me so much. I learned to make a meal seem effortless from Verna, how to enjoy entertaining from Jean, how to love God from my Nana, how to love people from my Mom, how to speak good about everyone from Shirley, how to be obedient to God even in difficult circumstances from my daughter.

So many women over the years have impacted my life with countless living examples.

Last chapter we looked at what older women need to be teaching younger women about loving their husbands, let's continue with this verse.

Titus 2:5 says,
"... to live wisely and be pure, to work in their homes, to do good, and to be submissive to their husbands. Then they will not bring shame on the word of God."

To '*live wisely*' is translated in other versions as '*to be self-controlled, to be discreet, to be virtuous.*' You get a clear picture of older women needing to teach younger women about living in such a way that is wise, with a sound mind and self control.

As you look over these scriptures write down why getting wisdom is so important in our lives and how we become wise.

Proverbs 1:5

Proverbs 2:11

Proverbs 12:16

Psalm 19:7

Psalm 119:24,98,100

Matthew 7:24

_____
_____
_____
_____

Titus 2:5 states that this training by '*older*' women needs to include teaching them '*to work in their homes, to do good and to be submissive to their* *husband*.' Many people have used this verse to put good Christian woman under a load of bondage that Paul never intended to happen with his letters.

Look at Galatians 5: 1-6

Although Paul is talking about putting new believers under the law of circumcision for men, he is also talking about living in bondage to the law.

Read this text and write down the contrasts of living according to rules and living according to the Spirit.

_____

_____

_____

_____

I have seen many extremes of the use of **Titus 2:5** and in the end, this was never meant to become a new law for women after the freedom that Christ had brought to both genders.

It is simply a new way of living in honoring God with our lives, in a place where it needs to be lived out in integrity, in our homes. In referring to this passage one Commentary wrote, 'The passage before us shows how much the honor of Christianity is bound up with the faithful discharge by Christians of the simple domestic duties of life. In truth, the family is the chief seat and often the main test of Christian virtue.'

In other words, how we treat those we live with is the strongest testing ground for the fruit of the Spirit to be revealed and grown in our lives. So older women are to encourage and teach younger women how to live out Christianity in their homes, to live in love and to be good to their husbands.

Look at the following scriptures to get an understanding of how God's Word describes a woman who doesn't know how to take care of her own home.

Proverbs 7:6-11

I Timothy 5:11-13

_____
_____
_____
_____

Describe after looking at these texts what God wants for our home.

Isaiah 32:18

Psalm 127:1,2

Proverbs 24:3-4

_____

_____

_____

_____

This teaching required a change of heart toward the most intimate of places, in our closest relationships, where the fruit of truly living in Christ would have its greatest effect. Older women were to teach younger women that they have now been given a new freedom in Christ and an example of how to live with those closest to them. This young Church and it's people needed to learn a new way of living, a Christ-centered way.

Look at these scriptures write down the things God is calling you to do, so you do not bring *'shame on the Word of God.'*

John 15:13

1 John 3:16

Ephesians 5:33

I Peter 5: 5-11

_____

_____

_____

_____

Desiring to grow in Christ, ask God to show you places in your heart where you can move from rebellion to humility and submission. Looking at the life of Jesus, see what He modeled, in how He lived in submission to His Father. As we seek to be like Him, living a life of submission to God and then making it a reality in our homes and workplaces, it gives us an opportunity to be more than hearers of the Word of God. It is in those places that we have the most opportunity to grow in the ways of God. It is learning every day how to lay down our desires for others. That's what making Jesus Lord of our life truly means!

Meditate on and memorize this verse:

Fear of the Lord teaches wisdom; humility precedes honor.
Proverbs 15:33

Chapter 9

Living As A Model of God's Grace

Show yourself in all respects to be a model of good works, and in your teaching show integrity, dignity, and sound speech that cannot be condemned, so that an opponent may be put to shame, having nothing evil to say about us.
Titus 2:7,8 ESV

For several years as a young girl and teen, I was a professional model for a chain of stores across the United States. On Monday's, I would work getting fitted for the designers clothing, and model them on Friday for the buyers. I got paid very well for the work that I did, although it was not as easy as it sounds. I mistakenly thought this would make me popular at school, but instead it made me the object of a lot of pain and torment. What I soon realized was, that being a model meant dealing with other people's jealousy and that I had to learn how to continue what I was doing under that torment.

In the English Standard Version, this text is translated *'be a model of good works,'* which we have been talking about as we have studied Titus.

'A model is something to be copied, one serving as an example to be imitated or compared'. Paul is saying here that we need to be models of good works in integrity, dignity and sound speech so that it will shame our opponents. The key here is that there will be people who oppose us, and we will have people to say evil about us, no matter how well we live but we need to continue to prove them false by our integrity and 'good works.'

As you read the following scriptures, write down what they are saying about how we are to *'model'* the teachings of Christ in the midst of people that may speak ill of us.

_____
_____
_____
_____

Does the way we live have an effect on the truth of the Gospel being revealed to others? Should our main concern be what others think of us?

1 Peter 2:11-12

2 Peter 2:2-3

2 Timothy 1:13-14

1 Thessalonians 2:10-12

Philippians 2:14-15

1 Corinthians 2:4-5

_____

_____

_____

_____

Titus 2: 11- 14

For the grace of God has appeared, bringing salvation for all people, training us to renounce ungodliness and worldly passions, and to live self-controlled, upright, and godly lives in the present age, waiting for our blessed hope, the appearing of the glory of our great God and Savior Jesus Christ, who gave himself for us to redeem us from all lawlessness and to purify for himself a people for his own possession who are zealous for good works.

Grace is unmerited favor that God so richly gives us and has pours out upon us through the gift of His own Son, Jesus Christ. This grace, and salvation so richly given to us when we didn't deserve anything, now teaches us how to live right.

Romans 5: 1-11 is one of the best scriptural explanations of Grace. Look at these verses and list what God has given us and what it does in our life.

The love of God constrains us not to live no longer for ourselves. When we truly come into a love relationship with God and see how much He has poured out His love and grace for us, it changes us and our lives are never the same. We begin to reflect that love in all we do.

Look at these verses and see what Christ's abundant love has done for us. How does that knowledge make you want to live?

2 Corinthians 5:14-15

1 John 4:17 - 19

Ephesians 5:1-15

Ephesians 4:20-24

_____

_____

_____

_____

What is God teaching you to renounce or to abandon as you embrace all that Christ has done for you?

_____

_____

_____

_____

Jesus has modeled for us how to live in an intimate relationship with God and how dearly loved we are. When we experience that kind of unconditional love, it should make us want to live our lives close to Him, following His example as a model for our lives. The purpose of His life and death was for us to be able to live close to God and rescued from destruction, living in the power of a resurrected life.

In these following scriptures, list what Christ has done for you and what your response should be.

John 1:14-18

John 5:19-23

2 Corinthians 8:9

1 John 3:1-6

1 Peter 1:3-9

Isaiah 25:9

Psalm 98:2-6

_____

_____

_____

_____

When we have been so dearly loved, so richly ransomed, and so abundantly filled with new life, we now have the gift of becoming models of Christ's love revealed to others. We get to reflect His love as we cast off things that weigh us down, just as you would an old piece of clothing that doesn't fit anymore. Then putting on a new garment, that Christ gives us as we respond to Him. We truly get to become super models of His life and grace! I am honored to say that is what I truly want to model now!

Years ago I wrote an article for a magazine and ended up on the cover, when I saw it for the first time, I could hear God's whisper to me, "I have called you to model the work of My Hand in your life, not the work of a man's hands." I realized at that moment what I had been truly called to do. May we all realize that as we walk closer to Jesus each day that we have the privilege of modeling what He is doing in and through our lives. That type of modeling has an eternal paycheck!

Ask the Lord to help you be truly grateful and aware of all that He has done for you that you can reflect what Christ has modeled for you.

_____

_____

_____

_____

Meditate on and memorize this verse:

Now may our Lord Jesus Christ himself and God our Father, who loved us and by His grace gave us eternal comfort and a wonderful hope, comfort you and strengthen you in every good thing you do and say. Thessalonians 2:16,17

Chapter 10

Humbled By God's Love

Remind them to be subject to rulers and authorities, to obey, to be ready for every good work, to speak evil of no one, to be peaceable, gentle, showing all humility to all men.
Titus 3:1 New King James Version

Since the fall of Adam and Eve in the garden, it is in human nature to rebel. I saw this clearly in my own life when we recently visited the museum. Although the thought had not previously been in my mind, when I saw the 'do not touch' sign near the marble statues, I suddenly wanted to touch them all! It was all I could do to contain myself from touching them. Then I realized; this was nothing but pure rebellion. The law brought out my own sin, and now I had to choose to obey the authority of those who wrote the sign and were prepared to enforce it.

Paul is now instructing Titus to remind believers to submit and be obedient to those in authority over us. Those two words, submit and obey, can be troublesome for us as adults. They are words we typically use regarding children and as adults we don't like to hear them. The truth is, we can be rebellious and disobedient as adults, and it crops up in many ways. One way I have seen this over and again is whenever we don't agree with the leadership in any arena. We can convince ourselves that we don't have to listen to them or follow what they say.

How do you react when those in authority over you ask you to do something? What if it is something you do not understand the same way they do?

_____

_____

_____

_____

I didn't comprehend why I couldn't touch ancient marble, after all it was a stone. But they did, and were asking me to obey them without that knowledge.

How do you respond when it is the Pastor of your Church?

_____

_____

_____

_____

In Chapter 3:1-2, Titus has instructions regarding how we relate to people in leadership over us. As you read the following scriptures write down who you are truly submitting to when you submit to leaders in place over you.

Exodus 22:28

1 Samuel 24:1-7

Hebrews 13:7, 17

Romans 13:1-2

1 Peter 2:13 - 23

_____

_____

_____

_____

Continuing in this chapter, directly after Paul addresses our relationship to leaders, he writes in verse three, *"Once we were foolish..."* reminding us that no matter how we feel about those in authority over us, we need grace to understand how to respond to authority. He then gives believers this poignant reminder: *"We used to live hating and being hated!"* This verse presents a graphic description of human depravity apart from Christ.

We can sometimes be lured into two extremes of thought regarding God's love and grace. We either find ourselves believing that we are too bad for God to love and bless us, or that we deserve His blessings because we have done everything right.

Look at Ephesians 2:1-10. Make a list of the ways God responds to us when we least deserve it and why.

_____

_____

_____

_____

Titus 3:4-5
But—"When God our Savior revealed his kindness and love, He saved us, not because of the righteous things we had done, but because of his mercy. He washed away our sins, giving us a new birth and new life through the Holy Spirit.

I am so very grateful for God's mercy and grace. Often, people ask me how I can have so much grace towards them, and my answer is always the same. " *I need so much grace in my life, I have to give it abundantly to others!"*.   **John 1:16** speaks to this exact thing.

As you study the following scriptures, what is God saying to you about His grace and mercy in your life and towards others.

Romans 5:20 - 6: 4

1 Timothy 1:12-17

2 Timothy 1:6-10

Luke 1:76-79

1 Peter 1:3-9

1 Corinthians 6:7 -11

_____

_____

_____

_____

Now as you pray, ask God to help you to be obedient and gracious to those in authority over you. Write down any insights that God reveals to you about obedience and submission during the next week. In a few months go back over this and see if there has been any real growth in this area.

May God pour out His abundant grace on you to walk away from the desire to rebel, as you consider all of His Love and mercy toward you. It is truly very humbling to realize that in all our ugliness He who knows all still loves us dearly. That is genuine grace!

Remember your leaders who taught you the word of God. Think of all the good that has come from their lives, and follow the example of their faith. **Hebrews 13:7** New Living Translation

Meditate on and memorize this verse:

When the law came into the picture, sin grew and grew; but wherever sin grew and spread, God's grace was there in fuller, greater measure. No matter how much sin crept in, there was always more grace.   Romans 5:20 The Voice Version

Chapter 11

Confidence In The Generous Love Of God

*He generously poured out the Spirit
upon us through Jesus Christ our Savior.*
Titus 3:6 *New Living Translation*

I will never forget the first time I left my children with a babysitter. I was genuinely concerned that the person I was leaving my precious children with not let them out of their sight and that they would be safe. Years later, when I was being prepared to babysit my grandson for the first time, my daughter had a list of things for me to know about caring for her child. I had to chuckle, because I had given the same type of list for the person who first cared for her when she was a baby. She had come from a Mom who knew all about leaving lists for people we trust to take care of our precious children!

When Jesus was about to leave this earth, He knew that he had come and broken the barrier between man and God. Through His death, He would re-establish the opportunity for intimacy with God. He could not leave God's dearly loved men and women alone without direct access to the presence of God. He had torn down the veil of separation, and now an intimacy with God was possible once again for every man and woman. This capacity and longing for intimacy was created in each of us from the beginning by God so that we could enjoy a deeper relationship with Him. The Holy Spirit has been given to each of us generously, abundantly and with constant accessibility. He is the one who today enables and empowers us to enjoy a deeper relationship with God. We have not been left alone and neglected!

Search the following scriptures and list what Christ has provided for us and how that should alter our daily life.

2 Corinthians 3:7-16

Ephesians 4:20-30

Romans 8:1-5

_____

_____

_____

_____

As followers of Christ, we can still find ourselves feeling insecure about our relationship and future with God. Most times as I have sat in Church or the presence of God, and I have felt overwhelmed by all of my shortcomings. Those thoughts are designed to completely disqualify me from God's presence because I begin falsely to think that His love is predicated on my performance.

Paul states clearly Titus 3:7

"Because of His grace He declared us righteous and gave us confidence that we will inherit eternal life."

We can have confidence today and in our future with God based on His grace and righteousness not ours.

Look at the following scriptures and write down any place of comfort God gives you in gaining confidence in your relationship with Him. Make a list as well of the ways that should effect how we live our lives each day.

I Corinthians 2:12

Romans 2:29

Romans 7:6

Ephesians 2:13-22

Galatians 2:19-21

Psalm 118:8

Philippians 3:7-11

_____

_____

_____

_____

The goal of all this teaching and training is wrapped up in Titus 3:8.

"This is a trustworthy saying, and I want you to insist on these teachings so that all who trust in God will devote themselves to doing good. These teachings are good and beneficial for everyone."

Devoting ourselves to doing good means that doing good for others needs to be a conscious, deliberate act of our will. It is too easy to go about our day and forget about anyone else and be completely self-focused. Later when we get alone with God finding ourselves feeling guilty as we realize places He might have wanted us to do good for someone else. We have to be willing to become deliberate about looking for opportunities for doing good. When we put this into our daily life, we become not just a hearer of

God's Word but a doer! Living right and doing good has been the central theme of the book of Titus - revealing to others that we have had sound teaching by how we treat them.

Write down attributes of a Christian towards the needy and what our actions should be towards others.

_____

_____

_____

_____

My hope is that as you look at these scriptures you will get a clear understanding of God's heart toward those in your world who are in need.

Matthew 25:37-46

Acts 20:35

Hebrews 6:10

Romans 12:9-21

Hebrews 13:2

Proverbs 14:31

Ephesians 4:32

Philippians 2:4

_____

_____

_____

_____

Today take some time to thank God for His generous love and mercy toward you. Ask Him to reveal your heart of gratitude to others in how you treat them, particularly strangers and the needy.

_____

_____

_____

_____

Meditate on and memorize this verse in the version of your choice:

It wasn't so long ago that we ourselves were stupid and stubborn, dupes of sin, ordered every which way by our glands, going around with a chip on our shoulder, hated and hating back. But when God, our kind and loving Savior God, stepped in, He saved us from all that. It was all His doing; we had nothing to do with it. He gave us a good bath, and we came out of it new people, washed inside

and out by the Holy Spirit. Our Savior Jesus poured out new life so generously. God's gift has restored our relationship with him and given us back our lives. And there's more life to come—an eternity of life! You can count on this. I want you to put your foot down. Take a firm stand on these matters so that those who have put their trust in God will concentrate on the essentials that are good for everyone.
Titus 3:3-8

CHRISTINA WILLIAMS

Chapter 12

Keep Doing Good!

This is a trustworthy saying, and I want you to insist on these teachings so that all who trust in God will devote themselves to doing good. These teachings are good and beneficial for everyone.
Titus 3:8 New Living Translation

I can remember sitting at a Weight Watchers meeting and seeing the teacher ring a bell every time they called the name of someone who had lost weight. The room would cheer, and they would continue to the next name. They repeated this every week, and it was a significant part of the meeting, it encouraged everyone else to hope that someday with hard work they would be the one receiving the cheers. It inspired everyone to keep up the good work.

Paul is finishing his letter to Titus with an encouragement to keep up the good work because it will be for the good of all and in the end we will hear the cheers of heaven.

He ends this letter as a warning of the activity that could derail this good work.

Titus 3: 9-11
Do not get involved in foolish discussions about
spiritual pedigrees or in quarrels and fights about
obedience to Jewish laws. These things are useless
and a waste of time. 10 If people are causing
divisions among you, give a first and second
warning. After that, have nothing more to do with
them. 11 For people like that have turned away
from the truth, and their own sins condemn them.

I find it fascinating that people that are divisive
and like to argue are referred in this text as those
who have turned away from the truth and will
have to deal with the condemnation of their own
sin. In the New Living Version, these people are
described as someone who is "sick with a love for
arguing and fighting about words." They are
people who just like to talk and talk, with no
resolve, and we need to be wary of getting
involved in this type of arguing.

**Look at what the scriptures say about how God
feels about this and how we are to treat these
people. Also, as you research these scriptures list
the characteristics of this type of person.**

I Timothy 1:7

1 Timothy 6: 1- 5

2 Timothy 2:14-19

2 Timothy 2:23-26

Romans 16:17

Proverbs 17:14

_____

_____

_____

_____

The words, 'avoid or reject' in some of the versions of **Titus 3:9,10** means to - 'shun or to refuse.' Too often we can find ourselves lured into conversations that become argumentative about foolish things, and they end up just a waste of time. Titus is being urged to shun this type of conversation, and the divisive people that start them, after warning them twice. So we are being encouraged to give these people an opportunity to stop, and if they insist, we need to draw the boundary before we get ensnared into their sin.

I can remember being involved in a conversation one time with a young theologian, and he wanted to argue about what would happen to someone in hell. It was clear he was just enjoying the argument and nothing would stop him being controversial and augmentative. I remember silently asking God to give me a word of wisdom (**1 Corinthians 2:13**) to get out of the conversation. I finally said, *"it doesn't matter to me what it will be like. I am going to focus my life and energy in the pursuit of never going there to find out!"*

Verse 11 describes this person as someone who has turned from the truth. In some versions, the word is translated subverted, but the word in the Greek is 'pervert.' They have perverted the truth into an argument or controversy. In the end, this type of person is very likely to be the one who ends up turning away entirely from God. The reason that they put themselves in danger of turning away from God is that they didn't enter into a love relationship with the Living God. They just wanted to argue with His people and be right!

Titus 3: 14
And let our people also learn to maintain good works, to meet urgent needs, that they may not be unfruitful.

Maintaining or practicing good works means that we keep at it, that it becomes a lifestyle of doing good for others. This type of lifestyle effects society in such profound ways that it is transforming to families, to communities and ultimately to the world.

Search throughout these scriptures for a practical view of how to maintain doing good on a daily basis.

Acts 20:35

Ephesians 4:28-32

1 Thessalonians 2:9-12

2 Thessalonians 3:7-13

Isaiah 61:1-3

_____

_____

_____

_____

The fruit of your walk as a Christian matters! Your life impacts others, and the fruit of how you live in Christ is significant to God. You are a vessel chosen by God to bear good fruit.

Look at the following verses and write down why it is significant that you 'maintain good works.'

Matthew 7:19-20

John 15:8

John 15:16

Colossians 1:9-12

_____

_____

_____

_____

May God give you great grace and wisdom as you walk in the places He has put you. As we conclude, pray that you will find grace to maintain a live of doing good in Christ. Ask someone in your life to hold you accountable to this, or to just pray for you to live in a way, that is pleasing to God.

_____

_____

_____

_____

Meditate on and memorize this verse:

And now, dear brothers and sisters, one final thing. Fix your thoughts on what is true, and honorable, and right, and pure, and lovely, and

admirable. Think about things that are excellent and worthy of praise. Keep putting into practice all you learned and received from me—everything you heard from me and saw me doing. Then the God of peace will be with you.
Philippians 4:8-9 New Living Version

I pray that the Lord will be kind to all of you!
Titus 3;15 Contemporary English Version

Grace (God's favor and blessing) be with you all. Amen.   Titus 3:15 Amplified Bible

NOTES

CHRISTINA WILLIAMS

_____

_____

_____

_____

_____

_____

_____

_____

_____

_____

_____

_____

_____

_____

_____

_____

_____

_____

_____

_____

_____

_____

_____

_____

_____

_____

_____

_____

_____

_____

_____

ABOUT THE AUTHOR

Christina Williams is the Founder and Director of Elevated to Excellence Women's Conferences. She is a dynamic speaker who has taught extensively in the U.S., Canada, Europe and other nations.

She has served with her husband, Grady, in pastoral ministry for over 30 years. Together they also teach 'The Secret To Enduring Love' marriage seminars.

They have two amazing adult children, a dearly loved son-in law and two incredible grandchildren.

CHRISTINA WILLIAMS

MINISTRY CONTACT INFORMATION

Contact Christina Williams at:

Email:
christina@elevatedtoexcellence.com

Website:
www.elevatedtoexcellence.com

You can also connect with her on:

Linkedin

Facebook

Twitter @ ElevatedtoE

18513421R00066

Made in the USA
San Bernardino, CA
17 January 2015